A PA<

Pride and Prejudice

Jane Austen

Abridged and adapted by Lisa Trumbauer
Illustrated by Matthew Archambault

Upper Saddle River, New Jersey
www.globefearon.com

Adapter: Lisa Trumbauer
Project Editor: David Cutts
Senior Editor: Lynn Kloss
Production Editor: Amy Benefiel
Marketing Manager: Kate Krimsky
Art Supervision: Angel Weyant, Eileen Peters
Art Coordinator: Cindy Talocci
Electronic Page Production: Leslie Greenberg, Lissette J. Quiñones
Cover and Interior Illustrator: Matthew Archambault

Copyright © 2001 by Globe Fearon Inc., One Lake Street, Upper Saddle River, New Jersey 07458. All rights reserved. No part of this book may be reproduced or transmitted in any form or by any means, electronic, photographic, mechanical, or otherwise, including photocopying, recording, or by any information storage and retrieval system, without permission in writing from the publisher.

Printed in the United States of America
1 2 3 4 5 6 7 8 9 10   04 03 02 01 00

ISBN: 0-130-23701-9

1-800-848-9500
www.globefearon.com

Contents

1. New Friends 1
2. At Netherfield 9
3. Wonderful Wickham 16
4. Love Found 24
5. Love Lost 31
6. A Surprise Proposal 37
7. Surprising Secrets 46
8. A Changed Man 55
9. A Runaway Bride 64
10. A Helping Hand 72
11. Bingley and Jane 78
12. Darcy and Elizabeth 85

Cast of Characters

Jane Bennet	The oldest of the five Bennet sisters.
Elizabeth Bennet	The second-oldest of the five Bennet sisters, also called Lizzy or Eliza.
Mary Bennet	The third-oldest of the Bennet sisters.
Catherine Bennet	The second-youngest of the Bennet sisters. She is also called Kitty.
Lydia Bennet	The youngest of the Bennet sisters.
Mrs. Bennet	The sisters' mother. Her only goal is to see all of her daughters married.
Mr. Bennet	The sisters' father.
Mr. Bingley	A new man in the neighborhood. He is single and has a lot of money.
Caroline Bingley	Mr. Bingley's sister. She is also called Miss Bingley.
Mrs. Louisa Hurst	Mr. Bingley's other sister.
Mr. Hurst	Louisa Hurst's husband.
Mr. Darcy	Mr. Bingley's good friend.
Georgiana Darcy	Mr. Darcy's much younger sister.
Mr. Collins	A distant cousin to the Bennets. He will inherit the Bennet estate.
Charlotte Lucas	A good friend of Elizabeth's.
Mr. Wickham	A man from the militia that is stationed in Meryton.
Lady Catherine de Bourgh	Mr. Collins's patroness and an aunt to Mr. Darcy.
Mr. and Mrs. Philips	An uncle and aunt to the Bennet girls. They live in Meryton. Mr. Philips works as a country lawyer.
Mr. and Mrs. Gardiner	An uncle and aunt to the Bennet girls. They live in London. Mr. Gardiner has his own business.

1 New Friends

It is exciting when a new man moves into a neighborhood. Especially if that man is single.

"My dear," said Mrs. Bennet one day. "Have you heard that Netherfield has been rented by a rich young man?"

"What is his name?" asked her husband.

"Bingley."

"Is he married or single?"

"Oh! Single, my dear! A single man with a large fortune. What a fine thing for our girls!"

"How so?"

"My dear Mr. Bennet," replied his wife, "I hope he will marry one of them."

"Has he moved here to find a wife?"

"Of course not! However, he may fall in love with one of them. You must visit him."

"Why don't you visit him? I will send a note with you. It will say that he can marry any of our girls. Although, I must throw in a good word for my little Lizzy."

"You will do no such thing. Lizzy is no better than the others. She is not as pretty as Jane or as good-natured as Lydia."

"They are all silly, but Lizzy has something more than her sisters."

"Mr. Bennet! How can you speak that way about your own children? You like to upset me. You have no feelings for my poor nerves."

"You are wrong, my dear. Your nerves are my old friends. You have talked about them for the past 20 years."

Mr. Bennet was a mix of humor and reserve. His wife did not understand him. All that she cared about was getting her daughters married.

Mr. Bennet did visit Mr. Bingley. Later, he thought that he would tease his family about it. "I hope Mr. Bingley will like your hat, Lizzy," he said.

"We cannot know what Mr. Bingley likes," said her mother. "You will not visit him."

"We shall meet him at the balls," said Elizabeth. "Mrs. Long has promised to introduce him."

"I do not believe Mrs. Long will do any such thing," Mrs. Bennet said. "She has two nieces of her own. Kitty! Stop coughing, for heaven's sake!"

"Kitty has no control over her coughs," said Mr. Bennet. He turned to his middle daughter. "Mary," he said. "What do you say about meeting Mr. Bingley? You are a lady of deep thought. You read many books."

Mary did not know what to say.

"Mary is thinking," he said. "Let us get back to Mr. Bingley."

"I am sick of Mr. Bingley," cried his wife.

"Why did you not say so? If I had known, I would not have visited him."

Their surprise was just what he hoped for.

"How good of you, my dear!" cried his wife. "How pleased I am!"

"Now, Kitty, you may cough," said Mr. Bennet, and he left the room.

"What a fine father you have, girls," said Mrs. Bennet. "Lydia, you are the youngest, but I think Mr. Bingley will dance with you at the next ball."

"I am the youngest," cried Lydia. "I am also the tallest."

Mr. Bingley went to London before the ball. When he returned, he brought a group of friends. Bingley's two sisters were with him. Also with him were the husband of the oldest sister and another man. The other man was named Mr. Darcy.

Mr. Bingley was good-looking. He behaved like a gentleman. He was very pleasant. His sisters were fine women. His brother-in-law, Mr. Hurst, was also a gentleman.

Bingley's friend, Mr. Darcy, however, drew everyone's attention. He was a fine, tall man. He had far more money than Mr. Bingley. The ladies said that he was much more handsome as well. For a time, he was admired in this way. However, he acted as if he were better than everyone else.

What a contrast between Mr. Bingley and his friend! Mr. Bingley soon knew everyone in the room. He was lively and open, and he danced every dance. He was upset that the ball was over so early. He talked of giving one himself. Mr. Darcy, however, danced only with Mrs. Hurst and Miss Bingley. He spent the evening walking around the room. Moreover, he spoke only to the Bingleys.

It was agreed: Mr. Darcy was the proudest, meanest man in the world. Everyone hoped he would never come again.

Elizabeth had been sitting down for two dances. She was close enough to overhear Mr. Darcy and Mr. Bingley talking.

"Come, Darcy, you must dance. I hate to see you all by yourself."

"I certainly will not. You know how I hate it unless I know my partner. Your sisters are already dancing. There is no other woman in the room that I care to dance with."

"What! I have never met so many pleasant girls in my life!"

"You are dancing with the only pretty girl here," said Mr. Darcy. He was looking at the oldest Bennet girl, Jane.

"She is the most beautiful creature I have ever seen!" agreed Bingley. "However, one of her sisters is sitting behind you. She is very pretty."

"Who do you mean?" Turning around, Mr. Darcy looked at Elizabeth. Then, he said coldly, "She is not too bad, but not pretty enough to tempt me."

Mr. Darcy walked off. Elizabeth later told the story to her friends. She loved anything ridiculous, such as Mr. Darcy's behavior.

The Bennets were in a good mood when they returned to their home in Longbourn. At the ball, Jane had been careful in her praise of Mr. Bingley. Now, however, Jane and Elizabeth were alone. Jane told her sister how much she liked him.

"He is just what a young man should be," said she. "He is sensible, good-humored, and lively."

"He is also handsome," replied Elizabeth.

"I was very flattered that he asked me to dance twice. I did not expect such a compliment."

"Why not? That is how you and I are different. Compliments always take you by surprise, and me never. Well, he certainly is very nice. I give you permission to like him. You have liked many stupider people."

"Lizzy!"

"It is true! You never see a fault in anyone. Everyone is good in your eyes. I never heard you say a mean word about anyone. What about his sisters? Their manners are not as nice as his."

"At first, no. However, they are very nice when you talk to them."

Elizabeth was not convinced. Mr. Bingley's sisters had not tried to be nice to anyone. They were fine ladies, but they were proud and conceited. They thought that they were better than other people.

Over the next two weeks, the Bennet and Bingley ladies visited each other often. Mrs. Hurst and Miss Bingley could not stand Mrs. Bennet. They thought that the younger Bennet girls were not worth speaking to. However, they wished to know Jane and Elizabeth better.

Elizabeth believed that Jane could easily fall in love with Mr. Bingley. However, Jane did not show her feelings. Elizabeth thought that Bingley might not know how Jane felt about him. Elizabeth was busy watching Mr. Bingley and Jane. She never suspected that she herself had become interesting to his friend.

At first, Mr. Darcy did not think that Elizabeth was pretty. The second time they met, he looked at her only to criticize her. Later, he began to notice her beautiful, dark eyes. Although her manners were not fashionable, he liked her easy playfulness.

Mr. Darcy wished to know Elizabeth better.

Elizabeth was totally unaware of this. To her, he was the man who was not nice to anyone. He was the man who had not thought her pretty enough to dance with.

One evening, the Bennets were at a ball at the home of their neighbors, the Lucases.

"My dear Miss Eliza," said Sir Lucas, "why are you not dancing? Mr. Darcy, allow me to present this young lady to you. You cannot refuse when so much beauty is before you."

Elizabeth drew back. "Indeed, sir, I do not care to dance."

Mr. Darcy then asked her himself. Elizabeth refused and turned away. She did not hurt Mr. Darcy's feelings. He was still thinking of Elizabeth when Miss Bingley walked up to him.

"I know what you are thinking," said Miss Bingley. "This is an awful evening. How annoying! These people are nothing! Yet they think they are important!"

"You are totally wrong. I have been thinking about the eyes of a very pretty woman."

"Indeed? Who is the owner of these fine eyes?"

"Miss Elizabeth Bennet," he replied.

"Miss Elizabeth Bennet!" repeated Miss Bingley.

Mr. Darcy listened without hearing a word.

2 At Netherfield

Mr. Bennet owned property that earned enough money to support him and his family. Unfortunately for his daughters, this estate would be inherited by a distant male cousin. If Mr. Bennet died, then Mrs. Bennet would not have enough money to support her daughters. Mrs. Bennet had a sister married to a Mr. Philips, who was a country lawyer. Mrs. Bennet's brother lived and worked in London.

The village of Longbourn was only one mile from Meryton. This short distance let the Bennet sisters visit their aunt, Mrs. Philips, three or four times a week. At the moment, they were very happy because a military regiment had just arrived. Meryton was its headquarters for the winter.

One day, a note came for Jane.

"Well, Jane, who is it from?" asked Mrs. Bennet. "What is it about? Well, Jane, tell us!"

"It is from Miss Bingley," said Jane, and she read it aloud.

> *My dear friend,*
> *If you do not visit us today, Louisa and I will be in danger of hating each other for the rest of*

our lives. A whole day between two women can never end without a fight. Come as soon as you can. My brother and his friends are having dinner with the officers in Meryton.

Yours ever,
Caroline Bingley

"Can I have the carriage?" Jane asked.

"No, my dear, you had better go on horseback," said her mother. "It looks like it is going to rain. Then you will have to stay all night."

"That would be a good plan," said Elizabeth, "if you were sure that they would not send her home in their own carriage."

"Oh! The gentleman will have taken the carriage to go to Meryton."

"I would much rather go in the coach," said Jane.

"My dear, your father cannot spare the horses. They are wanted at the farm, Mr. Bennet, are they not?"

"They are wanted at the farm more often than I can get them," he said.

Finally, Jane went on horseback, and her mother's hopes were answered. Jane had not been gone long when it rained. Her sisters worried about her, but her mother was delighted. It rained all evening.

"What a lucky idea I had!" said Mrs. Bennet.

The next morning, a servant from Netherfield brought a note for Elizabeth:

My dearest Lizzy,

I find myself sick this morning. I guess it is because I got soaking wet yesterday. My friends will not let me go home until I am better. They insist I see the doctor. However, except for a sore throat and headache, there is not much wrong with me.

Yours, etc.

"Well, my dear," said Mr. Bennet, "if your daughter should die, it should make you happy that it was all because of you."

"Oh! I am not at all afraid of her dying. People do not die of little colds. The Bingleys will take good care of her at Netherfield."

Elizabeth worried about her sister and wished to see her. The carriage was not available. Moreover, since she could not ride a horse very well, she walked. She crossed field after field and jumped over puddles. At last, the house came into view. Elizabeth had weary ankles, dirty stockings, and a face glowing with the warmth of her walk.

Her appearance created a great deal of surprise. It was incredible to Mrs. Hurst and Miss Bingley that she had walked three miles, but they were polite. Mr. Bingley was kind and with good humor.

Mr. Darcy said very little. He thought Elizabeth looked wonderful after her walk, but he wondered if she should have come so far alone.

Jane was happy to see Elizabeth, but she was not up to talking much. Elizabeth began to like Mrs. Hurst and Miss Bingley when she saw how much they cared for Jane. The doctor came, said that she had caught a bad cold, and told her to stay in bed. They took care of Jane for the rest of the day. Miss Bingley then invited Elizabeth to stay at Netherfield until Jane was better. Elizabeth agreed with thanks. A servant went to Longbourn to tell the news and bring back some clothes.

It was late in the evening when Jane finally slept, and Elizabeth went downstairs. The whole party was playing cards, and they asked her to join them. She said no, and said that she would amuse herself with a book.

"Mr. Darcy, what a great library you have at Pemberley, your estate!" said Miss Bingley.

"It should be good," he replied. "My family has worked on it for years."

"You have added so much to it yourself."

Elizabeth was so caught up in what they said that she laid her book aside.

"Has your sister, Miss Darcy, grown much since the spring?" said Miss Bingley. "Will she be as tall as I am?"

"I think she will. She is now about Miss Elizabeth Bennet's height, or rather taller."

"How I long to see her again!"

The next day passed much as the day before. Mrs. Hurst and Miss Bingley spent some hours in the morning with Jane, who was getting better. In the evening, Elizabeth joined them downstairs. Mr. Darcy was writing, and Miss Bingley was seated near him, watching. Mr. Hurst and Mr. Bingley were playing cards, and Mrs. Hurst was observing their game.

When he finished writing his letter, Mr. Darcy asked Miss Bingley and Elizabeth to play some music. Miss Bingley went quickly to the piano.

While Mrs. Hurst sang with her sister, Elizabeth could not help notice how often Mr. Darcy looked at her. She could not imagine that he liked her. The idea that he looked at her because he disliked her was even more strange. She could only think that there was something wrong with her. It did not bother her. She liked him too little to care.

When Miss Bingley began to play a lively song, Mr. Darcy went up to Elizabeth and said, "Do you feel like you want to dance?"

She smiled, but she did not answer.

He repeated the question.

"Oh, I heard you," she said. "But I did not know what to say. You wanted me to say, 'Yes,' so you could make fun of me. I like to upset those types of plans. I do not want to dance. Now you may dislike me if you wish."

"Indeed I do not."

Darcy had never been so bewitched by any woman. He believed that were it not for her poor relatives, he could be in danger of falling in love with her.

Miss Bingley saw enough to be jealous. She hoped that Jane would soon get well so she could get rid of Elizabeth.

The next evening, Elizabeth brought Jane downstairs, where she was welcomed by her two friends. When the gentlemen entered, Miss Bingley looked at Mr. Darcy. He spoke only to Jane. Mr. Hurst bowed slightly. Bingley was full of joy.

After talking with Jane, Elizabeth wrote to their mother the next morning to ask for the carriage so they could return home. Mrs. Bennet replied that they could not have the carriage before Tuesday. Nevertheless, Elizabeth was determined. She urged Jane to borrow Mr. Bingley's carriage.

Mr. Bingley was sad that they would soon leave. To Mr. Darcy, the news was welcome. Elizabeth attracted him more than he liked. He decided to be careful not to show how much he liked her. He barely spoke to her before she left.

Their mother did not welcome the girls' return. Their father, on the other hand, was very glad to see them. They found Mary, as usual, studying. Catherine and Lydia talked about the militia in Meryton.

3 Wonderful Wickham

The next morning, Mr. Bennet said, "A month ago I received a letter. It is from my cousin, Mr. Collins, who will inherit this house when I am dead."

"Oh!" cried his wife. "I cannot bear to hear about it."

"Nothing can clear Mr. Collins from the guilt of inheriting Longbourn," said Mr. Bennet. "However if you will listen to his letter, you may feel better."

Hunsford, near Westerham, Kent 15 October

Dear Sir,

The Right Honorable Lady Catherine de Bourgh has given me the position of minister of this town. As a clergyman, I feel it is my duty to bring peace to all families. Therefore, I hope that you will forget, for the moment, that I am next to inherit the Longbourn estate. I am concerned that this will hurt your daughters, and I apologize for it. I wish to make right this wrong. I would like to visit Longbourn on Monday, November 18, for one week. I remain.

Your friend,
William Collins

"If he wishes to help our girls," said Mrs. Bennet. "I shall not discourage him."

"I think he sounds strange," said Elizabeth. "I can't figure him out. There is something very conceited about him. What can he mean by apologizing for being next in line to inherit? Can he be a sensible man, sir?"

"No, my dear, I think not," said Mr. Bennet. "I hope he is quite the opposite."

Mr. Collins arrived on time and was welcomed politely. He was a tall, heavy young man of 25. He was serious and formal. He told Mrs. Bennet that she had a fine family of daughters. He added that he did not doubt that they would be married in time.

After dinner, Mr. Bennet spoke to his guest. He said that Mr. Collins seemed lucky to have such a friend as Lady Catherine. Mr. Bennet could not have chosen a better topic. Mr. Collins spoke very highly of her.

"Does she live near you?" asked Mrs. Bennet.

"My own garden is separated only by a lane from Rosings Park, where her ladyship lives."

"I think you said she was a widow, sir? Has she any family?"

"She has one daughter, the heiress of Rosings."

"Ah!" cried Mrs. Bennet, shaking her head. "Then she is better off than many girls. What sort of young lady is she? Is she pretty?"

"She is a most charming young lady. She is often ill, but she is very nice."

Mr. Collins wanted to marry, and he meant to choose one of the Bennet daughters. This was his plan for how to right the wrong for inheriting their father's estate. He thought it a good one and very generous on his part.

On the first evening of his visit, Jane was his choice. However, Mrs. Bennet told him that Jane was likely to be engaged soon. Therefore, he changed his mind from Jane to Elizabeth. Mrs. Bennet was happy that she might soon have two daughters married.

Soon after, Mr. Collins walked with the girls to Meryton. Here they met Mr. Denny, who was in the militia. Mr. Denny introduced them to his friend, Mr. Wickham, who had just joined the militia. Mr. Wickham was very handsome.

They were all standing and talking when they heard the sound of approaching horses. Darcy and Bingley rode up and began the usual hellos.

Bingley spoke mostly to Jane. Mr. Darcy was determined not to look at Elizabeth, but he was surprised to see Mr. Wickham. Elizabeth noticed that as the two men looked at each other, they were both shocked. Both changed color—one white, the other red. Mr. Wickham soon touched his hat and left.

What could it mean? Elizabeth was curious to find out more about these men.

That evening, the carriage took Mr. Collins and his five female cousins to the home of Mrs. Philips, the girls' aunt in Meryton. Mr. Wickham was also in the house.

While the others were playing cards, Mr. Wickham talked to Elizabeth. He asked how far Netherfield was from Meryton, and then he asked how long Mr. Darcy had been staying there.

"About a month," said Elizabeth. Unwilling to let the subject drop, she added, "He has a lot of property in Derbyshire, I understand."

"Yes," replied Wickham. "His estate, Pemberley, is a large one. I have known his family from the time I was a baby."

Elizabeth looked surprised.

"Do you know Mr. Darcy well?" Wickham asked.

"As much as I wish to," said Elizabeth. "I spent four days in the same house with him, and I think him very rude."

"I have known him too long and too well to be a fair judge," said Wickham. "Still, I believe your opinion would surprise others."

"Hardly! He is not liked at all in Hertfordshire. Everybody is disgusted with his pride."

"The world is blinded by his money. I wonder how long he will stay here."

"I do not know. I hope your plans will not change because of him."

"Oh, no. If he wishes to avoid me, *he* must go. We are not friendly, but I have no reason to avoid him. His father, the late Mr. Darcy, was my godfather. He thought that he had left me in good hands. It was his wish that, upon his death, a position would be found for me with the church. However, when a position was available, your Mr. Darcy gave it to someone else."

"Good heavens!" cried Elizabeth. "How could that be?"

"My godfather's wish was informal. A man of honor could not have doubted it. Yet your Mr. Darcy did."

"Why?"

"I believe he dislikes me. We spent the best part of our youth together. My father cared for the Pemberley property."

"How strange!" cried Elizabeth. "I wonder why Mr. Darcy's pride has not made him help you!"

"Pride has often been his best friend," replied Wickham.

"Could such pride do any good?"

"Yes. He is often generous. He gives his money freely and helps the poor. He has also brotherly pride, which makes him very kind and careful with his sister."

"What sort of girl is Miss Darcy?"

"I wish I could say she is nice, but she is too much like her brother—very, very proud. She is a pretty girl, about 15 or 16 years old."

"How can Mr. Bingley be friends with such a man? He cannot know what Mr. Darcy is."

"Probably not. However, Mr. Darcy can be a good friend if he thinks it is worth his while."

Mr. Wickham spied Mr. Collins, and he asked Elizabeth in a low voice if she knew the de Bourgh family.

"Lady Catherine de Bourgh has made Mr. Collins a minister of her town," she answered. "I don't know how Mr. Collins first met her, but he has not known her long."

"You know, of course, that Lady Catherine de Bourgh and Lady Anne Darcy were sisters. She is the present Mr. Darcy's aunt."

"I did not know that."

"Her daughter, Miss de Bourgh, will inherit a lot of money, and it is believed that she and Mr. Darcy will unite the two estates by getting married."

When Elizabeth left her aunt's home, she could not stop thinking of what Mr. Wickham had told her.

Later that day, Mr. Bingley and his sisters invited the Bennets to a ball at Netherfield. Elizabeth thought of dancing with Mr. Wickham, and of watching how Mr. Darcy reacted. She was so happy that she did not speak much to Mr. Collins. Therefore, she was surprised to learn that he would also be going to the ball.

"I take this opportunity, Miss Elizabeth, to ask for the first two dances with you," he said.

Elizabeth was shocked. She had imagined dancing with Wickham. It now struck her that *she* had been chosen by Mr. Collins to be his wife. Although her mother agreed with Mr. Collins's choice, Elizabeth chose to ignore it. Mr. Collins might never propose, and until he did, it was useless to think about it.

4 Love Found

Elizabeth never thought that Mr. Wickham might not go to the ball. She had dressed with great care and was hoping to win his heart. However, Mr. Denny said that Wickham had left the day before. He even hinted that Wickham had left so that he would not see Mr. Darcy.

This made Elizabeth dislike Mr. Darcy even more. However, she could not stay in a bad mood for long. She told everything to her friend, Charlotte Lucas, and they were soon talking about her strange cousin, Mr. Collins.

Elizabeth was horrified when she danced with Mr. Collins. He was awkward and serious, always saying that he was sorry instead of looking where he was stepping. Elizabeth was so embarrassed.

She danced next with an officer and had fun talking about Wickham and learning that everyone liked him. When those dances were over, she returned to Charlotte. Suddenly, Mr. Darcy asked her to dance. She was so surprised that, without thinking, she said yes.

For some time, they did not speak. Elizabeth began to think that they never would. Then, she decided that Mr. Darcy might like her less if she *did* talk. Therefore, she said something about the dance. He replied and was silent. Then, he asked if Elizabeth and her sisters walked to Meryton often. She told him yes, and added, "When you met us there the other day, we had just met someone new."

Mr. Darcy's face turned red, but he did not say a word. Finally, he spoke. "Mr. Wickham can easily *make* friends. If he can *keep* them is another story."

"He was unlucky to lose *your* friendship," replied Elizabeth.

Darcy did not answer. At that moment, Sir William Lucas appeared.

"Allow me to say, sir, that your partner is very pretty. I hope to have this pleasure often, especially when a certain event takes place." So saying, he glanced at her sister and Mr. Bingley.

Darcy seemed surprised, and he studied Bingley and Jane, who were dancing together. He then turned to Elizabeth and said, "Sir William has made me forget what we were talking about."

"I do not think we were speaking at all. We have tried two or three subjects without success. I cannot imagine what we will talk of next."

"What about books?" said he, smiling.

"I cannot talk of books in a ballroom. My head is always full of something else."

"Your mind is always on the present?"

"Always," she replied. Suddenly she exclaimed, "I understand that you hardly ever forgive. Once your anger is formed, it cannot be forgotten. You are careful, then, that it does not get formed?"

"I am," said he, with a firm voice.

"You are never blinded by prejudice?"

"I hope not. May I ask why you ask?"

"To better understand you."

"And?"

She shook her head. "I hear such different things about you, and they confuse me."

"I can believe it. I hope that you do not conclude anything about me right now."

She said no more, and when the dance ended, they went their separate ways. Neither was happy. Mr. Darcy's heart was flowing with feelings for her, but he was angry with someone else.

Soon, Miss Bingley came up. "Miss Eliza! I hear you like George Wickham! Your sister has been asking me a thousand questions. Let me suggest, as a friend, that you do not believe everything he has told you. Mr. Darcy has not treated him badly. In fact, he has always been very kind to him. It is George Wickham who has treated Mr. Darcy poorly."

Not wanting to believe it, Elizabeth went to find Jane. When she found her, she said, "I want to know what you have learned about Mr. Wickham."

"I have nothing good to tell you. Mr. Bingley does not know everything. However, he does stand up for his friend, Mr. Darcy. I am sorry to say that by his words, as well as his sister's, Mr. Wickham is not a man to be liked or trusted."

"Mr. Bingley does not know Mr. Wickham?"

"No."

"Then, what he knows is what Mr. Darcy has told him." With that, she was happy.

Elizabeth then listened to the happy hopes that Jane had for Bingley. Mr. Bingley soon joined them, and Elizabeth left to talk to Charlotte. Mr. Collins came up and told her that he had just learned that the nephew of Lady Catherine de Bourgh was at the ball.

"I must say hello to him."

Elizabeth tried to talk him out of it, but he would not listen. With a low bow, he left her to introduce himself to Mr. Darcy. Elizabeth watched as Mr. Darcy looked at Collins with surprise, then spoke to him with an air of distant politeness.

Mr. Collins was not the only member of Elizabeth's family to embarrass her. When they sat down to supper, Mrs. Bennet was talking to Lady Lucas about her hopes that Jane would soon be married to Mr. Bingley. She spoke very loudly. Most of what she said was overheard by Mr. Darcy. Elizabeth blushed and blushed again.

When supper was over, singing was talked of, and Elizabeth was mortified to see her sister Mary getting ready to sing. Mary sang one song and then began another. Her voice was weak. Elizabeth wanted to die. She looked at her father, who took the hint and kept Mary from singing yet another song.

Mr. Collins and the Bennets were the last to leave the ball. By a scheme of Mrs. Bennet's, they had to wait for their carriages 15 minutes after everyone had gone. Mrs. Hurst and her sister barely opened their mouths. Mr. Collins spoke long speeches. Darcy said nothing. Mr. Bennet, also silent, enjoyed the whole scene. Mr. Bingley and Jane stood together and talked only to each other.

The next day brought a new excitement to Longbourn. Mr. Collins proposed to Elizabeth.

"I wish to marry for three reasons," he told her. "First, because I think every clergyman should set the example. Second, I am sure it will make me happy. Third, Lady Catherine de Bourgh told me I should.

"You may ask why I have come to Longbourn to find a wife. I will tell you. Since I will inherit your father's estate after his death, I felt it best to choose one of his daughters for my wife. Now I must tell you how much I love you."

Elizabeth had to stop him.

"I have not given you an answer, sir. I thank you for thinking of me. However, I cannot marry you."

Mr. Collins said, "I understand that young ladies often say no to a man that they really like. Therefore, I still am hopeful."

"Mr. Collins!" cried Elizabeth. "I am not one of those young ladies, if such young ladies exist. I am serious! You could not make me happy. I am the last woman in the world who could make you so."

"The next time I speak to you about this," said Mr. Collins, "I hope to get a better answer."

"Really, Mr. Collins!" cried Elizabeth. "You puzzle me. I do not know what to say to convince you."

"I do not think that marrying me is such a bad thing," he explained. "My connections with the de Bourgh family, and my relationship to your own, are in my favor. In spite of your beauty, it is not certain that anyone else will propose to you because of your small inheritance. Therefore, I must conclude that you are not serious."

"I assure you, sir, that I am. I thank you, but to say yes is impossible."

"You are charming!" cried he.

Elizabeth left the room. Mrs. Bennet soon entered and congratulated him. Mr. Collins told her that Elizabeth had said no. Mrs. Bennet was shocked and surprised. She hurried to her husband.

"Oh! Mr. Bennet," she cried. "You must make Lizzy marry Mr. Collins. Tell her that you insist."

"Call her down," said Mr. Bennet.

When Elizabeth entered the library, her father said, "Come here, child. I understand that Mr. Collins has asked you to marry him. Is it true?" Elizabeth said that it was. "Very well," continued her father. "You have said no?"

"I have, sir."

"Very well," said Mr. Bennet. "Your mother, however, insists that you say yes. Am I correct, Mrs. Bennet?"

"Yes, or I will never see her again."

"An unhappy choice is before you, Elizabeth," said Mr. Bennet. "From this day you must be a stranger to one of your parents. Your mother will never see you again if you do not marry Mr. Collins. I will never see you again if you do."

Elizabeth smiled, but Mrs. Bennet was very disappointed. While the family was in this confusion, Charlotte Lucas came to spend the day. She was met by Lydia, who cried in a half whisper, "There is such fun here! Mr. Collins has proposed to Lizzy, and she will not have him."

A few minutes later, Mr. Collins took back his marriage proposal. Elizabeth had to listen to her mother's whining. Mr. Collins was stiff and silent. He barely spoke to her, and he spent the rest of the day with Charlotte.

5 Love Lost

The following day, a letter came for Jane from Netherfield. Elizabeth saw her sister's mood change. When they were alone, Jane took out the letter and said, "This is from Caroline Bingley. They have all left for London. They are not coming back."

Jane continued to read parts of the letter. Then, she said, "It is obvious that he will not be back this winter."

"It is only obvious that Miss Bingley does not want him to," said Elizabeth.

"Why do you think so? He does what he wants. The part that I am about to read, however, is the part that really hurts me."

Here, Jane read Miss Bingley's hopes that her brother would marry Mr. Darcy's sister, Georgiana. "What do you think of this, my dear Lizzy? Is it not clear? Caroline does not want me to marry her brother. She is convinced that her brother has no feelings for me. Can it mean anything else?"

"Yes, it can. Miss Bingley sees that her brother is in love with you, but she wants him to marry Miss Darcy.

She follows him to London to keep him there, and she tells you that he does not care about you."

Jane shook her head.

"Jane, believe me," said Elizabeth. "No one who has ever seen you two together can doubt how he feels. However, the case is this. We are not rich enough or grand enough for them. She wants her brother to wed Miss Darcy so that she may have less trouble marrying Mr. Darcy."

"You are wrong. Caroline cannot lie to anyone. I only hope that *she* is wrong."

The Bennets had dinner that night with the Lucases, and again, for most of the day, Charlotte spent time with Mr. Collins. This seemed very nice of her, but Charlotte's goal was to have Mr. Collins's love for herself. She was successful. Mr. Collins left the Longbourn estate in secret to speak with her, and soon it was settled. Sir William and Lady Lucas were quickly told, and they heard the news with joy. It was a great match for their daughter. Lady Lucas began to figure out how many years longer Mr. Bennet might live.

Charlotte had never thought highly of marriage, but it was the only choice for young women with little money. At the age of 27, and not being pretty, Charlotte felt that she was now lucky.

What she dreaded the most was telling Elizabeth, whose friendship she valued. She wanted to tell

Elizabeth herself, and she asked Mr. Collins not to hint at what had happened.

Therefore, it was not until after Mr. Collins had left the next day that Charlotte shared her news.

Elizabeth was shocked, but she wished her well.

"You must be surprised, because Mr. Collins had first wished to marry you," said Charlotte. "However, when you have had time to think it over, I hope you will agree with what I have done. I am not romantic, you know. I ask only for a comfortable home."

Afterward, Elizabeth was sitting with her mother and sisters, wondering if she should tell them, when Sir William Lucas himself came to share the news. At first, no one believed him. However, Elizabeth confirmed it and then offered her good wishes.

Nothing could console Mrs. Bennet. It took a week before she could see Elizabeth without scolding her. It took a month before she could speak to Sir William or Lady Lucas without being rude. It took many months before she could forgive her daughter.

Elizabeth felt that she and Charlotte could never be close friends again.

The only thing that was more upsetting was that Mr. Bingley had not come back. Eventually, a letter came from Miss Bingley. The first sentence explained that they were all in London for the winter. When Jane could read the rest of the letter, it was full of praise for Miss Darcy.

On the following Monday, Mrs. Bennet's brother and his wife came to spend Christmas at Longbourn. Mrs. Gardiner was younger than Mrs. Bennet and Mrs. Philips. She was a friendly, smart woman and a favorite with her nieces.

Mrs. Gardiner soon learned of the troubles that had fallen upon the girls. Elizabeth talked about Jane with Mrs. Gardiner, who then invited Jane to stay with them in London. Jane accepted gladly. She hoped, perhaps, to see Mr. Bingley.

The Gardiners stayed at Longbourn for a week. Mrs. Gardiner observed that Elizabeth and Mr. Wickham seemed to like each other. She decided to speak to Elizabeth about it.

"Please be careful," she said. "I have nothing to say against him. If he had his own money, a marriage might be perfect. As it is, you must not let your feelings run away with you."

"Do not worry," replied Elizabeth. "I will be careful. I am not in love with Mr. Wickham. However, he is the nicest man I ever saw. I do believe that it is smart not to get serious with him. Oh! That horrible Mr. Darcy!"

Mr. Collins returned soon after the Gardiners and Jane had left for London. This time he stayed with the Lucases. The day before the wedding, Charlotte paid a farewell visit, inviting Elizabeth to visit her in her new home in Kent.

The wedding took place. The bride and groom left for Kent. Elizabeth soon heard from Charlotte, and they wrote letters to each other often.

Jane had also written to tell them they had arrived in London safely. Elizabeth wanted to hear something of the Bingleys, but it was not until several letters later that Jane had news. "I did not think Caroline was in a good mood," she wrote, "but she was glad to see me and scolded me for not telling her that I was coming to London. I was right, then. My last letter must have gotten lost. I think I will see them again soon."

Elizabeth shook her head, convinced that only by luck would Mr. Bingley find out that Jane was in town.

Four weeks passed. Jane saw nothing of Bingley, and Caroline Bingley did not visit. When she finally did visit, the shortness of the visit and the change of her behavior was enough to convince Jane that she had been wrong. She wrote the following to Elizabeth:

My dearest Lizzy, I have fooled myself. Caroline did not visit me until yesterday. The visit did not make her happy. She said nothing about wishing to see me again. She cannot still think that her brother likes me. After all, if he did, we would have met by now. He knows I am in town, I am sure. I do not understand it.

I would almost think that she was lying to me. However, I will try not to think about it, and I will think only of things that make me happy.

Elizabeth felt bad for Jane, but at least Jane would no longer be made a fool. Elizabeth only thought the worst of Bingley. She hoped that he might marry Mr. Darcy's sister. According to Wickham, Miss Darcy would make him regret what he had thrown away in Jane.

As for Mr. Wickham, it seemed he now liked someone else—Mary King. The best thing about Miss King seemed to be that she had just come into a great sum of money.

Elizabeth then wrote to Mrs. Gardiner, "I am now convinced, dear aunt, that I have never been in love. Had I been, I would now hate the name Wickham. However, my feelings are not only kind toward him, but I feel nothing for Miss King. Kitty and Lydia take it much more to heart than I do. They are young and do not yet realize that handsome young men must have something to live on."

6 A Surprise Proposal

For the next few months, nothing much happened at Longbourn. In March, Elizabeth went to Hunsford with Sir William Lucas and Charlotte's sister, Maria, to visit Charlotte. They left early in the morning, and by noon they had reached London, where they visited Jane and the Gardiners. Elizabeth was happy to see that Jane was as healthy and as lovely as ever.

The next day, Elizabeth arrived at Hunsford. Charlotte, now Mrs. Collins, welcomed her friend with joy, and Elizabeth was very glad she had come. She saw that her cousin's behavior had not changed. He was just as odd as before. As he showed her around his home, she had only one thought. That thought was that he wanted her to see what she could have had if she had married him. Although everything was neat and comfortable, Elizabeth did not regret her choice. In fact, she was surprised that Charlotte could be so happy with such a husband.

About the middle of the next day, as Elizabeth was in her room getting ready for a walk, a sudden noise sent the whole house into confusion.

"Hurry!" cried Maria. "There is such a sight to see!" Elizabeth saw two ladies at the gate.

"Is this all?" cried Elizabeth. "I thought that the pigs were out in the garden."

"It is Miss de Bourgh and the old lady, Mrs. Jenkinson, who lives with them. Miss de Bourgh is a little creature."

"I like the way she looks," said Elizabeth to herself. "She looks sickly and mean. Yes, she will make Mr. Darcy a very good wife."

When the ladies drove on, Mr. Collins came inside with good news. They had all been asked to have dinner with Lady Catherine at Rosings the next day. Mr. Collins told them what they would see so that the sight of such rooms, so many servants, and so grand a dinner would not frighten them.

The next day, after a nice walk across the park, they climbed the steps to the hall of Rosings. They then followed the servants to the room where Lady Catherine, her daughter, and Mrs. Jenkinson were sitting. Her ladyship rose to greet them.

Lady Catherine was a tall, large woman, with strong features that might once have been pretty. When she spoke, the tone of her voice showed how important she thought she was.

Elizabeth then looked at her daughter. Miss de Bourgh was pale and sickly. She spoke very little except in a low voice to Mrs. Jenkinson.

The dinner was wonderful, and all of the servants and all of the china and food that Mr. Collins had promised were there. After dinner, there was little to do but listen to Lady Catherine talk. She gave her opinion on every subject, and it was clear that she was not used to having her opinions questioned.

Sir William stayed only a week, but it was long enough for him to believe that his daughter was doing well. Every few days, Mr. Collins walked to Rosings, and Charlotte went with him. Now and then, they were visited by Lady Catherine herself. She found fault with nearly everything, including the way the furniture was placed, how the maid worked, and the way the food was cut.

As for Elizabeth, she talked a lot with Charlotte, and the weather was so fine that she often went outside. Her favorite walk was along the open grove that edged the park. Here, she felt beyond the reach of Lady Catherine. In this quiet way, the first two weeks passed.

The week before Easter brought two visitors to Rosings—Mr. Darcy and his cousin, Colonel Fitzwilliam. Mr. Collins hurried to Rosings to welcome them. When he returned to Hunsford, he brought the two men back with him.

Colonel Fitzwilliam was about 30 years old, not handsome, but very nice, very polite, and spoke with ease. Mr. Darcy looked just as he had and spoke with his usual coolness. He sat for some time without speaking to anybody. After a while, his politeness returned, and he asked Elizabeth about her family. She answered him in the usual way, and after a slight pause, added, "My eldest sister, Jane, has been in London for the past three months. Have you not seen her?"

She did not think he had, but she wanted to see if he would tell her what had happened between Bingley and Jane. She thought that Mr. Darcy looked a little confused, but he answered that he had not seen Miss Bennet. The subject was dropped, and the gentlemen soon left.

A few days later, everyone at Hunsford was invited to Rosings. Colonel Fitzwilliam seemed glad to see them, for Elizabeth had caught his fancy. He now sat beside her, and they talked for some time. Mr. Darcy kept looking at them.

The next morning, Elizabeth was writing a letter to Jane. Charlotte and Maria had gone to the village, so she was alone when someone rang the bell. To her surprise, Mr. Darcy, and Mr. Darcy only, entered the room. He seemed just as surprised to find her alone, and he kept saying how sorry he was, for he had thought that Charlotte and Maria would be home, too.

They then sat down and seemed in danger of sinking into total silence. They talked for a bit about Charlotte and Mr. Collins and then about the area of Hunsford and Kent. Their talk soon ended when Charlotte and Maria came home. Mr. Darcy sat a few minutes longer without saying much, then went away.

"What can this mean!" said Charlotte as soon as he was gone. "My dear Eliza, he must be in love with you, or he would never have called on us in such a way."

Elizabeth denied it, yet as the days passed, Mr. Darcy and Colonel Fitzwilliam often came to visit. Colonel Fitzwilliam came because he liked their company. Why Mr. Darcy came was harder to understand. He would sit for ten minutes at a time without opening his lips. When he did speak, it seemed to be because he had to, not because he wanted to.

More than once, as Elizabeth walked within the park, she happened to meet Mr. Darcy, and she did not like it. She even told him that this part of the park was a favorite spot of hers, hoping that he would avoid it. Yet, he did not. He never said much, nor did she.

It was during such a walk when, instead of seeing Mr. Darcy, she saw Colonel Fitzwilliam. Their conversation soon turned to Mr. Darcy's sister.

"She is a friend of some ladies I know," Elizabeth said, "Mrs. Hurst and Miss Bingley. I think you might know them."

"I know them a little. Their brother is a great friend of Darcy's."

"Oh, yes!" said Elizabeth dryly. "Mr. Darcy takes a great deal of care of Mr. Bingley."

"Care of him? Yes! I believe he does! In fact, I think Bingley owes him."

"What do you mean?"

"Darcy told me that he saved a friend from a most unwise marriage. He didn't tell me who it was, but I think it was Bingley because they spent the summer together."

"Did Mr. Darcy explain?"

"He only told me what I have told you."

Elizabeth did not answer, but she became angry. She changed the subject until they reached the Collins's. There, she shut herself in her room so that she could think about what she had learned.

She had always thought that Mr. Darcy had come between Bingley and Jane. She had believed that Miss Bingley had come up with the idea. However, it had been Darcy. That Jane had been hurt was his fault. It was all because of Mr. Darcy's pride! He was afraid his pride would be hurt if his friend married a girl who had one uncle who was a country lawyer and another who worked in London.

Her tears gave her a headache. In addition, she did not want to see Mr. Darcy. Therefore, she decided not to go to Rosings with the Collinses that evening.

When the doorbell rang, Elizabeth hoped it might be Colonel Fitzwilliam. To her surprise, it was Mr. Darcy. He quickly asked about her health. She answered him coldly. He sat down for a few moments and then walked around the room. Elizabeth said not a word. Finally, he came toward her.

"I have tried to control myself," he began. He was very nervous. "I cannot. Please, you must let me tell you how much I love you."

Elizabeth was so shocked that she could not speak. She stared, blushed, thought that she must have heard him wrong, and was silent. Mr. Darcy went on. He spoke well, but he had more to explain besides the feelings of his heart. He also spoke of his pride. He believed that Elizabeth's family was too low for his family. His pride fought with what his heart felt.

Mr. Darcy then told her how much he loved her, even though he had tried to fight it. He hoped that she would marry him. Elizabeth could see that he did not doubt that she would say yes. The color rose into her cheeks, and she said, "In such cases, one should be thankful. If I could *feel* thankful, I would now thank you. However, I cannot. I have never tried to get you to like me. I am sorry to hurt you. I do not mean to, and I hope it will not last long."

Mr. Darcy was surprised. His face turned pale with anger. He tried to control himself, and he could not open his lips until then. Finally, in a voice of forced calm, he said, "Is this all I am to have? I might, perhaps, know why you say no."

"Then I will ask why you told me you liked me, even though you thought you shouldn't. That is not the reason. Mr. Darcy, do you think I could marry a man who has hurt my sister?"

Mr. Darcy changed color. Elizabeth continued.

"I have every reason in the world to dislike you. Nothing can excuse what you did. You were the one who split up Mr. Bingley and Jane, were you not?"

"Yes, I did, and I am happy for it. I have been kinder to *him* than I have been to myself."

"This is not the only thing," Elizabeth said. "I heard a story many months ago from Mr. Wickham. It showed the type of person you really are. Now what do you have to say?"

"You seem interested in his affairs," said Darcy in a less calm voice.

"How can I not be, when I know what you have done? He is poor because of you. You have kept from him the job that was planned for him. You have ruined his life. You have done all this!"

"This is what you think of me! Thank you for explaining it so well. My faults, according to you, are large, indeed! Perhaps you would not have thought so badly of me if *your* pride had not been hurt. You might not have said such bitter things if I had simply told you how much I loved you. I am not ashamed of my feelings. Could you expect me to be happy about your family?"

Elizabeth grew more and more angry, yet she tried to remain calm. "You are wrong, Mr. Darcy," she said. "The way you shared your feelings did not affect my answer. I still would have said no, but I might have been more kind if you had acted more politely—more like a gentleman."

He seemed surprised at this, but he said nothing, and she continued.

"You could not have proposed to me in any way that would have made me say yes."

"You have said quite enough, madam," said Mr. Darcy stiffly. "I understand how you feel. Forgive me for taking up so much of your time. I wish you good health and happiness."

With these words, he quickly left.

Elizabeth sat down and cried for half an hour. Mr. Darcy had proposed to her! He had been in love with her for months! He had been so much in love that he wanted to marry her—despite all of the things that had made him split up Bingley and Jane. She was flattered that he could love her so much. However, when she thought about his pride, she quickly forgot to feel sorry for him.

7 Surprising Secrets

The next morning, Elizabeth woke up with the same thoughts that she had fallen asleep to. She could not get over her surprise of Darcy's proposal, and she could not think of anything else. After breakfast, she went for a walk. Remembering that Mr. Darcy sometimes came to her favorite walking place, Elizabeth tried to avoid it so that she would not see him. It did not work.

He came up to her and gave her a letter.

"Will you please read that letter?" he asked stiffly. Then, with a slight bow, he turned again and was soon out of sight.

Elizabeth found two sheets of paper, covered in very small writing. The letter was dated from Rosings at eight o'clock that morning. It read as follows:

> *Do not worry, madam, that this letter is a repeat of my feelings or my proposal of marriage. I do not wish to cause you pain.*
>
> *You have accused me of two things. The first was that, no matter how they felt, I had split up Mr. Bingley and your sister. The other is that I had ruined Mr. Wickham. I hope you will*

change your mind when you read my story. If I happen to hurt you, I am sorry.

In Hertfordshire, I saw, like others, that Bingley liked your sister. At the Netherfield ball, I saw that his feelings for her were more than he had ever felt before. I also watched your sister. She was as cheerful as ever, but she did not seem to like Bingley in the same way. If I have been wrong and have hurt her, I understand your anger. However, there are other things I must tell you.

The total lack of manners of your mother, your three younger sisters, and even your father was a concern. I am sorry. It hurts me to hurt you. The fact that you and your sister were so well liked, despite your family, is praise. I believed that if my friend were to marry your sister, he would be unhappy.

When Bingley left Netherfield, he was going to come back. However, his sisters and I talked. We joined him in London, and I told him what I have just told you. He might still have come back if I had not shared with him my belief that your sister did not like him. I am not sorry that I did this. However, I do admit that I did not tell him that your sister was in town. I thought he might still like her, and to see her would hurt him. If I have hurt your sister, I did not do it on purpose.

As for Mr. Wickham, I can only tell you the whole story. I am not sure exactly what he has said. However, I shall tell you the truth, which others can also tell you.

Mr. Wickham is the son of a man who for many years worked at Pemberley, which is my family's estate. My father paid for the son to go to school. My father was very fond of this young man, who was also his godson. He hoped that he would work in the church, and he planned for Wickham to have such a job.

My father died five years ago. In his will, he asked if I would take charge of Mr. Wickham's employment, and he hoped that a position in the church would be found. He was also to inherit a certain amount of money from my father. Mr. Wickham's own father did not live much longer. Within half a year, Mr. Wickham wrote to me. He said that he had decided not to go into the church. He said that he wanted to study law, but the interest earned on the money he inherited from my father was not enough to support him. He asked if I would give him some additional money instead of helping him to find a position in the church. I agreed. Mr. Wickham signed away my help in the church. In return, I gave him three times as much money as my father had left him.

However, he did not study law, and he lived an idle life. I heard little of him for about three years. When the clergyman that Wickham would have replaced died, Wickham again asked for the position. He told me that things were bad. He found that he could not make money at law. You could hardly blame me for saying no. He was very angry with me, and he spoke badly of me to others.

I did not see him again until last summer. I must now tell you something that is hard for me. Please do not tell anyone.

My sister, Georgiana, who is more than ten years younger than I, was left in the care of Colonel Fitzwilliam and myself. About a year ago, she was sent to a school in London. Last summer, she went to Ramsgate, a seaside resort, with the lady who was in charge of the school. Mr. Wickham followed. It seems that the lady, Mrs. Younge, was an old friend of Wickham's. Wickham began courting Georgiana, who believed she was in love with him and wanted to elope. She was only 15. I caught up with them, and she told me all. You may imagine what I felt and how I acted. Because of my sister, I did not tell anyone. Mr. Wickham only wanted my sister's money. I wonder if he also hoped to get revenge on me.

This, madam, is the true story of everything that has happened. If you do not believe me, you can ask Colonel Fitzwilliam.

God bless you.
Fitzwilliam Darcy

Elizabeth did not know what to feel. At first, she was prejudiced against everything that he had written. She read and reread the letter. She put it down and thought about everything. Then, she picked it up and read it again. In every line, there was another side. At one point, she almost asked Colonel Fitzwilliam about it, but she thought that would be too strange.

She remembered everything that she and Wickham had said that first night at Mr. Philips's. She was now struck with how wrong it was of him to tell her, a stranger, such things. Why did she not think of it before? She remembered how he had boasted that he was not afraid to see Mr. Darcy, yet he did not go to the Netherfield ball. She remembered also that as soon as Mr. Darcy had left Hertfordshire, Wickham had told his version of the story to everyone.

How different it now seemed!

"How horrible I have been!" she cried. "I could not have been more blind had I been in love. Pride, not love, has been my folly. I was happy because Mr. Wickham seemed to like me. I was angry because Mr. Darcy would not dance with me or talk to me. I have been so stupid. Till this moment, I never knew myself."

She read again Mr. Darcy's explanation about Jane and Bingley. Of course, he was right. Jane *had* hidden her feelings. When she came to the part about her family, she was even more ashamed. She had felt the same way about their behavior at the ball. His kind words about herself and Jane were fine. However, they did not make her feel better.

Mr. Darcy and Colonel Fitzwilliam left Rosings the next morning. Elizabeth was also to leave soon. Lady Catherine gave them advice about when they should leave, how they should travel, how they should pack, and where they should stop.

After a six-week stay at Hunsford, it was finally time to go home. Elizabeth and Charlotte hugged warmly, and Mr. Collins walked Elizabeth to the carriage. Maria was already inside.

"Good gracious!" cried Maria as the carriage set off. "It seems only a day or two since we first came! So much has happened."

"A great deal, indeed," said Elizabeth with a sigh.

"How much I shall have to tell!"

Elizabeth said to herself, "How much I shall have to keep a secret."

Within four hours, they reached Mr. Gardiner's house in London, where they stayed a few days.

Jane looked well, but Elizabeth wanted to watch her more closely at Longbourn.

It was the second week in May when the three young ladies set out for Hertfordshire. Mr. Bennet's carriage met them at an inn, where they were greeted by Lydia and Kitty. After a quick bite to eat and a lot of chatter, the ladies were again on their way. Lydia had also shared with them the news that the militia would soon be leaving Meryton to go to Brighton. Elizabeth could not have been happier. She knew that Mr. Wickham would be leaving with the militia.

"Now, I have some more news for you," Lydia continued. "It is about dear Wickham. He is not going to marry Mary King!"

"Mary King has been saved from an unwise marriage," said Elizabeth.

"She is a fool if she really liked him," said Lydia. "I was hoping that one of you would have a husband before you came home. Jane is almost 23! How ashamed I would be if I were not married by 23! How I would like to be married before any of you. Then, I could chaperone *you* to the balls!"

Elizabeth spoke to Jane the morning after they arrived home. Jane was at first surprised to learn of Darcy's marriage proposal. She was sorry for the pain that Elizabeth's refusal must have given him.

"Do you blame me for having spoken so well of Wickham?" asked Elizabeth.

"I am sure that whatever you said was not wrong," replied Jane.

"It was!" She then told Jane about the letter.

Jane, who always tried to see the good in people, was shocked. "I do not know when I have been more surprised. Wickham so very bad! It is beyond belief! There is such goodness in him."

"Something went wrong in the raising of these two men. One is very good, and the other only acts like he is good."

"How unlucky that you spoke so strongly to Mr. Darcy," said Jane.

"I know," replied Elizabeth. "I have been prejudiced toward him from the beginning. Do you think that we should tell anyone about Wickham?"

Jane paused, then said, "Surely there is no need. What do you think?"

"I think that we should not. Mr. Darcy has not told me that I could tell others. Anyway, Wickham will soon be gone."

"You are right. This could ruin Wickham forever."

Elizabeth had now told two of her secrets, but there was still one more. She could not tell her sister that Mr. Bingley had had feelings for her. After watching Jane, Elizabeth could tell that she still had feelings for him.

8 A Changed Man

They had been home for two weeks. Now it was the last week of the militia's stay in Meryton. All of the young ladies were disappointed. Mrs. Bennet shared their sadness.

"If only we could go to Brighton!" she said.

"Oh, yes!" cried Lydia, "but Papa is so mean."

Lydia's gloom was soon cleared away. She was invited by Mrs. Forster, the wife of the colonel of the militia, to go to Brighton. Elizabeth thought it would be foolish for Lydia to go. She asked her father to forbid it. She told him that she thought Lydia could get into real trouble and that she would disgrace the family. Mr. Bennet did not take Elizabeth's warning too seriously.

Elizabeth had her own trip to look forward to. Her aunt and uncle, the Gardiners, had invited her to take a trip with them to the lakes. It was the only thing that made Elizabeth happy. If she could have included Jane in the plan, it would have been perfect. Two weeks before they were to leave, a letter arrived from Mrs. Gardiner. Due to business, Mr. Gardiner would not be able to leave, and the time would now be too short to go to the lakes. The new plan was to go only as far as Derbyshire. Mrs. Gardiner found the trip exciting, because she had once lived there.

Elizabeth had set her heart on seeing the lakes. Derbyshire brought many other ideas. Each time she thought of Derbyshire, she thought of Pemberley and its owner, Mr. Darcy.

After seeing all of the main wonders of the country, they wound their way to the little town of Lambton, where Mrs. Gardiner once lived. Within five miles of Lambton was Pemberley. Mrs. Gardiner and her husband wanted to see it.

Elizabeth was upset. She felt that she had no business at Pemberley, and she tried to change their minds. She said that she was tired of visiting great houses. Mrs. Gardiner still wanted to see the place.

Elizabeth could not agree to the plan. The very thought of accidentally meeting Mr. Darcy was awful! She blushed at the very idea. That evening, she talked to the maid at their inn about Pemberley and asked if the family was in town. When the maid said no, Elizabeth felt relieved. Now she could safely agree to visit Pemberley.

The estate was very large. They drove for some time through a beautiful forest. Elizabeth saw and loved it all. After about half a mile, they found themselves at the top of a hill, where the woods ended and the house sat on the other side of a valley.

It was a large, handsome, stone building backed by woody hills and with a stream in front.

Upon entering the house, the housekeeper came to give them the tour. Mrs. Reynolds was an older woman. They followed her into the dining room. It was large and had fine furniture. Elizabeth went to a window to see the view. The hill, crowned with woods, was beautiful. Every part of the grounds was good. Elizabeth looked as far as she could see—the river, the trees on its banks, the winding valley—and was delighted. The rooms were large and handsome, and the furniture was perfect. Elizabeth admired the owner's taste, for it was neither gaudy nor useless. It had less splendor but more elegance than the furniture at Rosings.

"Of this place," she thought, "I might have been mistress!"

She wanted to ask if the owner was really absent, but she did not have the courage. Her uncle did. Mrs. Reynolds replied, "We expect him tomorrow with a group of friends."

Mrs. Gardiner now called Elizabeth to look at a picture. It was of Mr. Wickham. The housekeeper told them that the picture was of the son of the late owner's caretaker. "I am afraid that he has turned out very wild," she added. "That picture," she said, pointing to another painting, "is of the new owner."

"I have heard that he is a fine man," said Mrs. Gardiner. "He is handsome. Lizzy, you can tell us whether or not it looks like him."

"Does the young lady know Mr. Darcy?"

Elizabeth blushed. "A little."

"Do you not think him very handsome?" asked the housekeeper.

"Yes, very handsome."

Mr. Gardiner's manners were easy and pleasant. He asked questions, and Mrs. Reynolds enjoyed talking about Mr. Darcy and his sister.

"Is Mr. Darcy at home much during the year?"

"Not so much as I would like."

"If he would marry, you might see more of him."

"Yes, sir, but I do not know when that will be. I do not know who is good enough for him."

Elizabeth could not help saying, "It is very nice that you think so."

"I say no more than the truth. I have never heard a harsh word from him in my life. I have known him ever since he was four years old."

Elizabeth wanted to hear more. She was grateful when her uncle said, "There are very few people of whom so much can be said."

"I do not think I could ever meet with better. He is the best landlord and the best employer. Some people call him proud, but I never saw it. I believe it is only because he does not rattle away like other young men."

In the gallery hung many family portraits. Elizabeth looked for one of Mr. Darcy. He had such a smile on his face—one she had sometimes seen when he looked at her. She felt better toward him than she had before. The praise from Mrs. Reynolds was huge. As a brother, a landlord, and an employer he was responsible for so many people's happiness! As Elizabeth gazed at his portrait, she thought of his feelings for her with deeper gratitude.

After leaving the house, they walked across the lawn toward the river. Elizabeth turned back to look at the house again. Suddenly, Mr. Darcy himself came from the road that led to the stables.

Their eyes met, and they both blushed. He seemed frozen with surprise, but he came up and spoke to Elizabeth. If he was not perfectly in control, he was perfectly polite.

Elizabeth was very embarrassed. She was surprised and confused and could barely lift her eyes to his face. She was not even sure what she said to him. Eventually the conversation ended, and he left.

Elizabeth felt ashamed. She should never have visited Pemberley! He had acted so differently! What could it mean? That he could even speak to her was amazing! He was so polite! He had even asked about her family! Never in her life had she seen him so kind.

Elizabeth did not know what to think. They continued their tour of the grounds. After some time, she was surprised to see Mr. Darcy again. He asked if she would do him the honor of introducing her friends. He was now asking to know those very people that his pride had warned him about when he had proposed to her.

Elizabeth was almost certain that Mr. Darcy would quickly leave when he learned who they were. However, he walked back with them and began speaking with Mr. Gardiner. Elizabeth listened to everything they said. She gloried in every smart sentence from her uncle.

The conversation soon turned to fishing. She heard Mr. Darcy invite her uncle to fish at Pemberley as often as he liked. Elizabeth's shock was complete. She kept asking herself, "Why has he changed? It cannot be for me. It is impossible that he should still love me."

They walked for some time with the two ladies in front and the two men behind. Then, Mrs. Gardiner wanted to walk with her husband. Mr. Darcy took her place. After a short silence, Elizabeth spoke first. She wanted him to know that she had thought that he was not at home. He then told her that Bingley and his sisters would arrive the next day.

"There is also one person," he said after a pause, "who I would like you to meet. Will you let me introduce you to my sister? Do I ask too much?"

This was one of the nicest things he could have asked her. The next day, Mr. Darcy did indeed bring his sister to the inn where Elizabeth and the Gardiners were staying.

Elizabeth was very nervous. She was afraid that Mr. Darcy might have said too many nice things about her to his sister. She wanted to please, but she was afraid that she would fail.

Elizabeth was surprised to see that Miss Darcy was as embarrassed as she was and very shy. She was tall and a bit bigger than Elizabeth. At 16 years old, she was very womanly and graceful. Elizabeth sensed good humor in her.

Soon after they had arrived, Bingley entered. Elizabeth was no longer angry with him. He asked about her family, and he was as easy as ever. Elizabeth thought of her sister, and she wondered if he was also thinking of Jane. Bingley and Miss Darcy did not seem to be in love with each other as Caroline Bingley had hinted. In fact, Bingley said a few things that led Elizabeth to believe that he still cared for Jane.

Mr. Darcy acted just as he had the day before. He was so nice and so eager to please.

They stayed for about half an hour. Before leaving, Mr. Darcy invited Elizabeth and the Gardiners to dine at Pemberley before they left the country.

Mr. and Mrs. Gardiner could think only good things about Mr. Darcy. Their friends in Lambton said only good things, as well. They said that he did much good for the poor. As for Mr. Wickham, it was known that when he left Derbyshire, he owed a lot of money. Mr. Darcy had paid Wickham's debts.

A new idea also came to them. As they watched Mr. Darcy, it became clear that he was in love with their niece. How Elizabeth felt was not so obvious.

Elizabeth lay awake for two hours that night trying to sort out her feelings. She did not hate Mr. Darcy. In fact, she felt more friendly toward him after his new behavior. Above all, she was thankful. She was grateful that he had once loved her and that he seemed to love her still. He seemed to have forgiven the way that she had spoken to him. She had thought that he would avoid her. Instead, he still wanted to be friends.

9 A Runaway Bride

Two letters came from Jane at the same time. Elizabeth began the first letter, which started with tales about parties. The end of the first letter, which was dated a day later, had more important news.

Something bad has happened, Lizzy. A letter came at twelve last night from Colonel Forster. Lydia has gone off to Scotland to marry Wickham! Imagine our surprise. Kitty, it seems, knew about it. I am so, so sorry. I hope that you can read this. I'm not sure what I have written."

Elizabeth quickly read the other letter. It had been written a day later.

By this time, you should have received my first letter. Dear Lizzy, I have bad news, and it cannot wait. Even though a marriage between Mr. Wickham and Lydia would not be smart, we now are afraid that it has not taken place at all. Colonel Forster came yesterday. He heard that Wickham never intended to marry Lydia, and he tried to find them, but he had no luck. The last time they were seen was on the road to London.

I do not know what to think. We are all so upset. Father and Mother believe the worst.

Mother is sick and stays in her room. As for Father, I have never in my life seen him so worried. Moreover, he is angry at Kitty for hiding what she knew.

I did not want to do this, but I can't help it. Please come home as soon as you can. Father is going to London with Colonel Forster to try to find Lydia. I am not sure what he wants to do, but he is so angry that he may do something foolish. We need our uncle's help.

"Oh, where are they?" cried Elizabeth, for Mr. and Mrs. Gardiner had gone for a walk. As Elizabeth darted to the door to find them, Mr. Darcy came in. "Please excuse me, but I must find Mr. Gardiner right away."

"What is the matter?" cried Mr. Darcy. "Let me or a servant go after Mr. and Mrs. Gardiner. You are not well enough to go yourself."

Elizabeth's legs began to shake, and she knew that she could not go after them. Breathlessly, she asked the servant to fetch the Gardiners home.

Elizabeth then sat down. She looked so worried that Darcy could not leave her. "What can I do for you? A glass of water—shall I get you one? You look very sick."

"No, thank you," she replied. "There is nothing wrong with me. I am upset by some horrible news from Longbourn."

She burst into tears, and for a few minutes she could not speak a word. Darcy could only watch. Finally, she spoke. "I have just had a letter from Jane. My youngest sister has left all of her friends—has eloped—has thrown herself at—at Mr. Wickham. They have gone off together. *You* know him too well. She has no money—nothing that can tempt him. She is lost forever."

Darcy was too surprised to speak.

"When I consider," she added, "that *I* might have prevented it! *I*, who knew what he was. Had I told some part of what I knew, this would not have happened. Now it is too late."

"Are you sure?" cried Darcy.

"Oh, yes! They left Brighton on Sunday night and were tracked almost to London."

"What has been done?"

"My father has gone to London, and Jane has written to ask for my uncle's help. We will leave, I hope, in half an hour. It does not matter. How will they be found? I have no hope."

Darcy did not answer. He walked up and down the room, deep in thought. His air was gloomy. Elizabeth thought she understood why. Here was proof of how bad her family could be. She did not blame him. For the first time, she felt that she could have loved this man.

However, she could not think about herself—only Lydia. Mr. Darcy told her that he would keep what had happened a secret. He told her how sorry he was. With one last look, he went away.

As soon as the Gardiners returned, they were on the road to Longbourn. They traveled quickly, and by sleeping one night on the road, they got to Longbourn by dinner the next day.

Jane met them at the door, and then they went to see Mrs. Bennet, who met them with tears and moans. She blamed everybody but the person who had made her daughter the way she was—herself.

In the afternoon, Jane and Elizabeth talked about what had happened. Jane explained that Lydia had written to Kitty, telling her that she might do such a thing. Kitty knew that Lydia and Wickham had fallen in love while in Brighton. She had also learned that Wickham owed money in Meryton.

"Oh, Jane, if we had not kept secret what we knew about Wickham, this would not have happened!"

"Perhaps," said Jane. "However, to tell someone's mistakes seemed wrong. We did what we thought was right."

Everyone hoped that a letter would come from Mr. Bennet the next morning, but the mail came without a single line. Mr. Gardiner had waited only for the mail, and then he set off.

Everyone in Meryton now talked badly about Mr. Wickham. He owed money to every shop in town. Everyone said that he was the most wicked young man in the world and that they had never trusted him.

Mr. Gardiner had left Longbourn on Sunday. On Tuesday, his wife received a letter from him. It explained that he had found Mr. Bennet but that Lydia and Mr. Wickham had not been found. The next plan was to write to Colonel Forster and to find out from some of Wickham's friends if he had any relatives who might know where he could be.

Every day was full of worry—mostly when waiting for the mail. Mr. Gardiner wrote again when he had an answer from Colonel Forster, but the news was not good. No one knew if Wickham had a single relative. Mr. Wickham had left gambling debts behind. Colonel Forster believed that a great deal of money would be needed to pay his debts in Brighton. Mr. Gardiner added that Mr. Bennet would return on Saturday. Mrs. Gardiner would then return to London when Mr. Bennet came back.

When Mr. Bennet arrived, he said very little and did not mention Lydia. It was some time before Elizabeth felt brave enough to speak of it.

"You must not be too hard on yourself," she said.

"No, Lizzy, let me, for once in my life, feel how much I am to blame. You were right in your advice last May." He added that he would not let the same thing happen to Kitty. She would be allowed to go out only with her sisters.

Two days after Mr. Bennet returned, a letter came from Mr. Gardiner.

> *My dear Brother,*
>
> *At last, I can send you some news. Soon after you left on Saturday, I was lucky to find Lydia and Mr. Wickham. I have seen them both. They are not married. However, if you are willing to do a few things, it should not be for long.*
>
> *All you need to do is to give your daughter her share of the money that she will receive when you die. You must also agree to give her during your life a small amount of money each year.*
>
> *On your behalf, I have agreed to these terms. I am also happy to say that there will be some money left over even when all of his debts have been paid. If you let me act in your name, I will get everything ready. Stay at Longbourn. Send your answer as soon as you can. We think it best that Lydia should stay with us. She will arrive today.*
>
> *Yours, etc.*
Edw. Gardiner

"Will he really marry her?" cried Elizabeth.

"Wickham is not so bad as we have thought," said Jane. "Congratulations, Father."

Elizabeth asked, "Must you agree to the money terms?"

"Agree to!" said Mr. Bennet. "I am ashamed that he asked for so little. I want to know two things. One, how much money did your uncle pay to make this happen? Two, how will I ever pay him back?"

"What do you mean?" cried Jane.

"I mean that no man in his right mind would marry Lydia with so little money offered."

"That is true," said Elizabeth. "It must be my uncle! A small sum could not do all this."

"No," said her father. "Wickham is a fool if he takes her for less than twice as much money."

Elizabeth and Jane then went upstairs. Mrs. Bennet was overjoyed by the news. Lydia was going to be married and that was all that mattered.

Mrs. Bennet was now busy looking for a proper home for her daughter and son-in-law without even thinking of what their income might be.

Her husband let her talk. When they were alone, he said, "Mrs. Bennet, before you choose a house for your daughter and son-in-law, understand this. Into *one* house they shall never be welcome. I will not encourage their behavior by welcoming them at Longbourn."

Mrs. Bennet was then amazed to learn that her husband would not give any money to buy new clothes for his daughter. She was more bothered by the disgrace of Lydia's not having new clothes than the shame of Lydia's having run off with Wickham.

Elizabeth thought about Mr. Darcy. Even if Lydia's marriage had happened the right way, she still did not think that Mr. Darcy would want to be connected with a family that was now connected with a man he disliked so much.

She now understood that Mr. Darcy was the best man for her. It was a marriage that would have been good for both of them. Her lively spirit might have softened his mind and his knowledge would have improved hers.

Mr. Gardiner soon wrote again, and he told them that Mr. Wickham was going to quit the militia, go into the regular army, and be stationed in the north. Mrs. Bennet was not happy that Lydia would be so far away.

His daughters asked that Lydia be allowed to visit before she set off. At first, Mr. Bennet said no. Eventually, however, he agreed to welcome them as soon as they were married.

10 A Helping Hand

Their sister's wedding day arrived, and the happy couple came to Longbourn. Mrs. Bennet smiled, Mr. Bennet looked angry, and her sisters were worried and uneasy.

Lydia's voice was heard in the hall, the door was thrown open, and she ran into the room. Her mother stepped forward, hugged her, and welcomed her happily. Mrs. Bennet then gave her hand with a warm smile to Wickham.

Mr. Bennet did not welcome them quite so politely. He barely opened his lips. In fact, the easy way the young couple acted made him angry. Elizabeth was disgusted, and even Jane was shocked.

Lydia was still Lydia—wild, noisy, and fearless. She went from sister to sister and demanded that they congratulate her. When she finally sat down, she laughed and said that it had been a long time since she had been there. The bride and her mother could not talk fast enough.

Wickham was as nice as ever. He sat near Elizabeth and asked about his friends. Both he and Lydia seemed to have the happiest memories in the world.

Elizabeth could not stand it. She got up and left the room. She went back only when it was time for dinner. She watched as Lydia said to Jane, "Now I get to sit next to Mother because I am a married woman. You must sit lower down the table."

The couple stayed for ten days. Mrs. Bennet and her daughter talked, and Mrs. Bennet threw several parties. The parties were fine with everyone. They were better than having family evenings alone.

Wickham's feelings for Lydia were just what Elizabeth had thought—he did not love Lydia as much as Lydia loved him. He was her "dear Wickham" all of the time.

One morning, when Lydia came upon Elizabeth and Jane, she said to Elizabeth, "Lizzy, I never told *you* about my wedding. Aren't you curious?"

"Not really," replied Elizabeth.

"You are so strange!" cried Lydia. "Nevertheless, I must tell you. We were married at St. Clement's, you know. We were all to be there by 11:00 A.M. On Monday, we ate breakfast at 10:00 A.M. as usual. I thought it would never be over. My uncle and aunt were so mean when I was with them. I did not once put my foot outside even though I was there for two weeks. Well, just as the carriage came to the door, my uncle had to leave. I was so frightened, for my uncle was to give me away. If we were late, we could not be married. Luckily, he came back again in time, and then we set out. Then, I remembered that if he *had* been late, the wedding could have taken place anyway, for Mr. Darcy could have taken his place."

"Mr. Darcy!" cried Elizabeth.

"Oh, yes! He came with Wickham. Oh, no! I forgot! I was not supposed to say a word about it. I promised them! What will Wickham say?"

"If it is a secret," said Jane, "say not another word. We will not ask about it."

"Of course not," said Elizabeth, though she was burning with curiosity.

"Thank you," said Lydia, "for then I would have to tell you everything, and then Wickham would be angry."

Mr. Darcy had been at her sister's wedding! It was exactly at a place and exactly among people where he would not want to be. Ideas about what it could mean rushed through her brain, but none made sense. Therefore, she wrote a short letter to her aunt. As soon as she got a reply, she hurried outdoors where no one would bother her as she read it.

My Dear Niece,
I have just received your letter, and I shall try to answer your questions. On the day that I arrived from Longbourn, Mr. Darcy came to visit. He and your uncle talked for several hours. He told your uncle that he had found your

sister and Mr. Wickham. From what I know, he left Derbyshire a day after we did to look for them. He blamed himself for what had happened. He blamed his pride for not letting anyone know the kind of person that Mr. Wickham really was. He thought it was his duty to fix this evil.

It took him several days to find them. They had been helped by a Mrs. Younge. His first goal was to ask Lydia to leave and return to her friends. He even offered his help. Lydia said that she did not care for her friends, she wanted no help from him, and she would not leave Wickham.

Since she felt this way, Mr. Darcy felt it was wise to speed up the marriage. He learned in his first talk with Wickham that marriage had never been his plan. Wickham said that he was going to resign from the militia because of some gambling debts. As for the future, he could not think about it. Mr. Darcy asked why he had not married your sister. Mr. Wickham said that he still hoped to make money through marriage— perhaps in some other country. He would, though, accept some help right now. They talked about it several times, and Wickham wanted more money than he could get, but finally it was worked out.

Mr. Darcy's next step was to tell your uncle, which he soon did.

Mr. Darcy was very stubborn. I think, Lizzy, that being stubborn is his real fault. Everything that was decided with Wickham, Mr. Darcy did. I am sure that your uncle would have done so, too. They argued for a long time, but at last, your uncle agreed. He was forced to take the credit, which he did not like. However, I think that your letter pleased him, because it forced you to know the truth. Yet, Lizzy, this must go no farther.

In spite of all this, your uncle would never have agreed if we did not think Mr. Darcy had another interest here. Mr. Darcy agreed to be in London when the wedding took place, and all money matters would be settled.

I believe I have now told you everything. Will you be very angry with me, my dear Lizzy, if I tell you how much I like him? He needs nothing but a little more liveliness, and that, if he marries wisely, his wife may teach him. Forgive me if I guess too much. I write no more. The children have been wanting me for a half-hour.

Yours, very sincerely,
M. Gardiner

Elizabeth was not sure if she was happy or hurt. Mr. Darcy had done all this for Lydia, a girl he did not like. Elizabeth's heart whispered that he had done it for her. This hope soon faded when she thought about her new family member: brother-in-law Wickham! Darcy's pride would hate the thought!

They owed Mr. Darcy everything. How bad she felt for every cruel thing she had ever thought and every hurtful speech she had ever said to him. She was proud of him. Proud that he had been able to think beyond himself. She read over her aunt's praise of him. It was hardly enough.

Suddenly, she was met by Wickham. They spoke for a few minutes, and he seemed to want to defend his actions to her. Unwilling, for her sister's sake, to upset him, she only said, "Come, Mr. Wickham. We are brother and sister now. Do not let us fight about the past. In the future, I hope that we shall always agree."

11 Bingley and Jane

When Lydia left, Mrs. Bennet was very sad for days. However, she was soon cheered by some news. The maid at Netherfield was getting the house ready for the Bingleys.

Jane could not hear of it without blushing. "I saw you look at me today, Lizzy, and I know I looked upset, but I was only confused. I knew that everyone would look at me. I tell you, the news does not make me happy or sad."

Elizabeth still thought that Bingley had feelings for Jane. In spite of what Jane said, Elizabeth could see that she was more nervous than usual.

On the third morning after Bingley's arrival at Netherfield, he came to Longbourn. Elizabeth looked out of the window and, to her surprise, saw Mr. Darcy with him!

"Mr. Darcy!" said Mrs. Bennet. "Well, any friend of Mr. Bingley's is welcome here. However, I must say that I hate the very sight of him."

Jane looked at Elizabeth with surprise and concern. To Jane, he was the man whom Elizabeth had refused. To Elizabeth, he was the person who had secretly helped the whole family. She also had feelings for him like those Jane had for Bingley.

The color that had left her face returned for half a minute with a new glow, and a smile of delight made her eyes sparkle when she thought that he still might care for her. She concentrated on trying to stay in control.

Jane looked a little pale. When the men came in, her color got brighter, yet she was polite. Elizabeth said as little as possible without being rude. She glanced only once at Darcy. He looked as serious as ever. Bingley looked both happy and embarrassed. Mrs. Bennet welcomed him with warmth, yet she greeted his friend coolly. Elizabeth, who knew what her mother owed to Mr. Darcy, was hurt for him. Yet, during the visit, he spoke not a word.

As soon as they were gone, Elizabeth walked outside. Mr. Darcy confused her. She asked herself, "Why did he come if only to be silent? Why can he be friendly to my uncle and aunt but not to me? If he fears me, why come? If he no longer cares for me, then why not say a word?"

Jane's reaction was different.

"Now that the first meeting is over," said she, "I feel better. I shall never be embarrassed again by seeing him. I am glad that he is having dinner here on Tuesday. Then, everyone will see that we are only friends."

"Oh, Jane, be careful," said Elizabeth, laughing.

"My dear Lizzy, you cannot think I am in danger now."

"I think that you are in danger of making him love you as much as ever."

On Tuesday, a large group met at Longbourn. When Darcy and Bingley went to the dining room, Elizabeth watched to see where Bingley would sit. He paused. When Jane looked around, then smiled at him, it was decided. He sat beside her.

This was the only joy Elizabeth would have. Mr. Darcy was almost as far away from her as could be. He was at the opposite end of the table on one side of her mother. She knew how little this would please either of them. She was not near enough to hear what they said, but she could see how little they spoke to each other. Her mother's behavior made what they owed him even more painful. She hoped that later she would have a chance to talk with him. However, it was not to be.

After everyone had left, Jane said to Elizabeth, "It has been a very nice day. I hope that we meet again often."

Elizabeth smiled.

"Lizzy, stop it!" cried Jane. "I enjoy talking to Mr. Bingley without hoping for anything else. I am happy that he never had any serious thoughts about me."

"You are very mean for not letting me smile when you are so funny," replied Elizabeth.

"Why is it so hard to believe? Why do you think I feel more than I do?" asked Jane.

"Forgive me," Elizabeth replied. "If you insist on saying that you two are just friends, then do not tell me your secrets."

A few days after this visit, Mr. Bingley called again, and he was alone. Mr. Darcy had left that morning for London, but he would return in ten days. Mr. Bingley went to Longbourn again the following day, and he stayed for supper. Before he went away, plans were made with Mr. Bennet to go hunting the following morning.

After this, Jane said no more about being just friends.

Bingley and Mr. Bennet spent the morning together, and Mr. Bennet was much friendlier than Bingley had expected. He was more talkative and less odd than before. Bingley returned with him for dinner, and in the evening, Mrs. Bennet saw to it that Bingley and Jane were left alone.

Upon entering the room, Elizabeth saw her sister and Bingley standing together near the fireplace and talking. Their faces quickly turned, and they moved away from each other. Elizabeth felt very awkward. She was about to leave when Bingley whispered a few words to her sister and ran out of the room.

Jane came up, hugged her sister, and said that she was the happiest person in the world. Bingley had asked her to marry him. Elizabeth said how happy she was for her.

"I must tell Mother," she cried. "I would not want her to hear it from anyone but me. He has gone to talk to Father already. Oh! Lizzy, to know that I can make my family so happy!"

It was a happy evening for all. Jane's face glowed so sweetly that she looked more beautiful than ever. Kitty smiled and hoped that her turn was coming soon. Mrs. Bennet could not show her happiness warmly enough. Mr. Bennet's mood showed how happy he was.

"Oh! My dear, dear Jane," cried his wife. "I am so happy! I always said it would be so. I was sure that you could not be so beautiful for nothing! I remember that when Mr. Bingley first came to Hertfordshire last year, I thought you should get together. Oh! He is the most handsome young man that ever was seen!"

Wickham and Lydia were forgotten. Jane was by far her favorite child.

From this time on, Bingley came to Longbourn every day. Elizabeth now had little time to talk to her sister. However, one evening, Jane said to her, "Do you know, Bingley told me that he did not know that I was in London last spring!"

"I thought so," replied Elizabeth. "How did he explain it?"

"It must have been his sisters' doing. They certainly were not happy with me, which does not surprise me, for he could have chosen someone much better than me. However, when they see that their brother is happy, they will get used to it. We shall be on good terms again, though we can never be as close as we once were."

"Why, Jane! That is the most unforgiving speech I ever heard you say. Good girl!"

"Imagine," said Jane, "that when he went to London last November, he really loved me. However, he thought that I did not like him!"

"He made a little mistake."

Elizabeth was pleased to find that he had not told Jane what Mr. Darcy had done. Although Jane could be forgiving, Elizabeth knew that this would prejudice her sister against Darcy.

The Bennets were quickly said to be the luckiest family in the world. Only a few weeks before, when Lydia had first run away, they had been thought to have no luck at all.

12 Darcy and Elizabeth

One morning, about a week after Bingley and Jane were engaged, a carriage pulled into the drive. It was Lady Catherine de Bourgh. She was ruder than usual. She wished to speak to Elizabeth alone.

"I am sure you know why I am here, Miss Bennet," she began coldly.

Elizabeth was surprised. "Indeed, I have no reason for the honor of your visit."

"Miss Bennet," she replied in an angry tone, "I have been told that not only is your sister to be married, but that *you*, Miss Bennet, will soon be married to my nephew, Mr. Darcy. Do you pretend not to know?"

"I never heard it before." Elizabeth blushed.

"Has he made you an offer of marriage?"

"Your ladyship has said that it is impossible."

"It should be, if he is sane. But *you* may have made him forget what he owes his family. Mr. Darcy is engaged to *my daughter*."

"Well, if he is, you have no reason to think that he will propose to me."

Lady Catherine paused, and then said, "From the time that they were born, they have been meant for each other. It was his mother's wish. Are they now to be prevented by a young woman of no importance? Have you not heard me say that he was to marry my daughter?"

"Yes, but what is that to me? If Mr. Darcy has no feelings for her, why can he not make another choice? If I am that choice, why can I not say yes?"

"Stubborn girl! I am ashamed of you! Tell me once and for all. Are you engaged to him?"

"I am not."

Lady Catherine seemed pleased. "Will you promise never to become so?"

"I will make no such promise."

"Miss Bennet, I am shocked. I had hoped to find a more reasonable young woman. However, I will not go away till you have told me what I need to hear."

"I never will."

Lady Catherine would not give up. "I know about your youngest sister and Wickham," she said. "Is such a girl to be my nephew's sister? Is her husband, the son of his late father's steward, to be his *brother?* What are you thinking?"

"You *now* have nothing else to say," said Elizabeth hotly. "You have insulted me."

"You refuse, then, to agree. You want to ruin him. Very well. I know now what I must do."

Not many days passed before Mr. Darcy returned from London, and he and Bingley visited Longbourn.

During a walk, Elizabeth and Darcy found themselves alone. Elizabeth needed to speak to him.

"Mr. Darcy, I must thank you for your kindness to my sister. Ever since I have known, I have wanted to tell you how grateful I am. If the rest of my family knew, they would feel the same. Let me thank you again and again in the name of all my family."

"If you thank me, let it be for yourself alone. I only wished to make you happy. Your family owes me nothing. I thought only of you."

Elizabeth was too embarrassed to say a word.

After a short pause, Mr. Darcy said, "You are too kind to play with my feelings. If you still feel the same as you did last spring, tell me at once. My feelings and wishes have not changed. One word from you, and I will never mention it again."

Elizabeth told him that her feelings had changed. She loved him, and she wished to accept his proposal of marriage.

Mr. Darcy had never felt happier. He told her so as warmly and as sensibly as a man in love could do. Elizabeth soon learned that they owed it all to Lady Catherine, who *had* visited him.

"Her visit gave me hope," he said. "I knew that if you still disliked me, you would have told Lady Catherine so."

Elizabeth blushed and laughed. "Yes, you know how truthful I can be."

"What did you say that I did not deserve? Thinking about how I acted is painful to me now. I shall never forget your words: 'If you had acted more like a gentleman.'"

Darcy then mentioned his letter. "Did it make you think better of me?"

She said that it had.

"I have been a selfish person all of my life," he said. "As a child, I was taught what was right. I was given good principles, but I followed them with pride. As an only son, I was spoiled by my parents, who taught me to think meanly of the rest of the world. I might still be that way if not for you, dearest, loveliest Elizabeth! You taught me a lesson. You humbled me."

"I am almost afraid to ask what you thought when we met at Pemberley. Did you blame me for coming?"

"No, I was only surprised."

"Not as much as I," said Elizabeth.

"I wanted to show you that I was not so mean as to resent the past. I also wanted you to forgive me and to not think so badly of me by letting you see that your words had been heard."

He then told her how happy Georgiana had been to meet her. Elizabeth also learned that Darcy had decided to look for her sister as soon as he had left the inn that day and that he had been silent because he was trying to decide how best to help.

Their thoughts soon turned to Bingley and Jane. Darcy said, "I told Bingley that I was mistaken in thinking that your sister had no feelings for him. I also told him that your sister had been in London three months last winter, and that I had hidden it from him. He was angry, but he has since forgiven me."

They continued talking until they reached the house, where they parted.

That night, Elizabeth opened her heart to Jane. Jane did not believe it. "You are joking, Lizzy. This cannot be! Engaged to Mr. Darcy! Impossible."

"This is terrible! If you do not believe me, nobody will. Yet, it is the truth. He still loves me, and we are engaged."

"My dear, dear, Lizzy. I—I congratulate you—but are you sure? Forgive the question—are you sure that you can be happy with him?"

"Without a doubt. But, are you happy, Jane? Will you like to have Mr. Darcy as a brother?"

"Very much. Nothing could make Bingley or myself happier. Do you really love him?"

"Oh, yes! It happened so slowly that I hardly know when it began."

The next morning, Mrs. Bennet stood at the window and said, "Oh, my! Mr. Darcy is coming again with our dear Bingley! Why does he come here all the time? What shall we do with him? Lizzy, you must walk with him again so that he is not in Bingley's way."

Elizabeth could hardly help laughing, but it still bothered her that her mother always gave him such a hard time. During their walk, they decided that they would ask for Mr. Bennet's consent that evening. Elizabeth would tell her mother.

Darcy followed Mr. Bennet to the library that night. Elizabeth was all nerves. She did not fear that her father would say no. She was afraid that *she,* his favorite child, would upset him by her choice of a husband. Mr. Darcy appeared again, and she felt better by his smile.

"Your father wants you in the library," said Darcy.

Her father was walking about the room looking worried. "Lizzy, what are you doing? Are you out of your mind to accept this man? Have you not always hated him?"

"I love him," she replied, with tears in her eyes. "In fact, he is very kind. You do not know what he is really like."

"Lizzy," said her father, "I gave him my consent. However, please think about it. I know you, Lizzy. I know that you could never be happy if you did not like your husband."

Eventually, Elizabeth convinced her father. She then told him what Mr. Darcy had done for Lydia.

"So, Darcy did everything," he exclaimed. "Made the match, gave the money, paid the debts, and got him a new job! This will save me a world of trouble and money. Had it been your uncle, I would have paid him. However, young lovers want everything their own way. I shall offer to pay Darcy. He will rant about his love for you and that will be the end of it."

Next, Elizabeth told her mother. At first, Mrs. Bennet was unable to make a sound. Then, she began to fidget in her chair, get up, sit down again, wonder, and bless herself. She was so in awe of Mr. Darcy that she could not even speak to him.

Happy was the day that Mrs. Bennet said goodbye to her two most deserving daughters. I wish I could say that her daughters' good marriages made her a sensible, well-informed woman for the rest of her life. However, they did not.

Mr. Bennet missed his second daughter very much. He loved going to Pemberley—especially when he was least expected.

Mr. Bingley and Jane remained at Netherfield for only a year. Jane's mother and her Meryton relatives were too nearby. Mr. Bingley bought an estate near Derbyshire, and Jane and Elizabeth were within 30 miles of each other.

Kitty spent most of her time with her two elder sisters. Away from Lydia, she was less whiny.

Although Lydia often invited Kitty to stay with her, Mr. Bennet would never allow it. Mary was the only daughter who stayed at home.

Over time, Wickham and Lydia grew to have no feelings for each other. Darcy would never welcome Wickham at Pemberley, but Lydia sometimes came to visit. For Elizabeth's sake, Darcy did continue to help Wickham in his work.

Miss Bingley was mortified by Darcy's marriage. However, she still wanted to visit Pemberley, so she accepted it. She was very fond of Georgiana, and she treated Elizabeth politely.

Georgiana thought very highly of Elizabeth. At first, she was surprised by how Elizabeth could tease her brother. With Elizabeth's help, she learned that a woman could have fun with her husband, which a brother will not always allow with a sister who is more than ten years younger.

Lady Catherine was still angry. In her letter to Darcy she used such nasty language that they did not speak for some time. Eventually, however, Darcy asked for a truce.

With the Gardiners, they were always friends. Darcy and Elizabeth really loved them. They felt the warmest gratitude for the two people who, by bringing Elizabeth to Derbyshire, had brought them together.